YOUNG WRITERS

SAFARI

SOMERSET

Poetry Now
YOUNG WRITERS

Edited by Lucy Jeacock

First published in Great Britain in 1997 by
POETRY NOW YOUNG WRITERS
1-2 Wainman Road, Woodston,
Peterborough, PE2 7BU
Telephone (01733) 230748

HB ISBN 1 86188 286 6
SB ISBN 1 86188 281 5

FOREWORD

Poetry Now Young Writers was established in 1992, with the aim to motivate and promote creative writing by young people. The *Safari* competition certainly achieved this aim, as our office was turned into a jungle of rhymes, ditties and limericks over the past few months!

It was encouraging to discover that a great deal of effort and attention to detail was put into each entry. The content was extremely varied; from complex environmental issues, to humorous poems about what is lurking in the cupboard! This made the arduous task of editing the poems submitted worthwhile.

The variety of subjects and styles chosen for *Safari Somerset* are an insight into today's generation and hopefully we can all learn from their beliefs.

CONTENTS

THE POEMS

Time

Time
I'm travelling through a time zone
With ticking going through my mind
A tree has caught my eye
Its leaves growing and then dying
Every second
All time is a black and white place
With no colour

That's all time really is
A mystery.

Daniel Hinton (10)
All Saints CE VA Primary School

River

Slow flowing long river
Billions of little drops racing to the sea
I lean against a little tree watching the
massive waters flowing to the sea
Fish make ripples in front of me
I feel drowsy in the hot sun
I long for a drink but this water is too muddy
Sadly I leave the river and head for home.

Richard Smith (11)
All Saints CE VA Primary School

DOES ANYONE CARE?

I hate it here
It is cold and damp
I hate the food
It is bread and water
I wash all the clothes
There are rats in my bedroom
My bedroom is in the attic
I get whipped too
Does anyone care?

Harriet Brookman (8)
All Saints CE VA Primary School

STORM

Once it was a stormy day
I wish I could go out to play
The rain was flowing down the street
As all together drops did meet.
We watched the lightning from our house
We sat as quiet as a mouse
I longed for the sun to come out today
Looks like I will have to play another day.

Adam Warner (11)
All Saints CE VA Primary School

Slave Work

I'm sweating
I'm hot and tired
I want to go to sleep
I want to see the master
I want to snap the chains.

Stuart Sloan (8)
All Saints CE VA Primary School

No Freedom

I am a slave
No freedom for me
I am starving
I get whipped to death
I am struggling for survival.

Jamie Harley (9)
All Saints CE VA Primary School

It's Unfair

From in amongst the bamboo,
the pandas stare and look at you.
They don't know what's happening,
don't know why they're dying.
Isn't it bad?
We never feel sad.

It's not fair
we don't need their hair
If we're not there to give them bother,
they will play like sister and brother.
They'll soon be extinct,
Now, what do you think?

Emma Harris & Keira Pearce (11)
Avishayes County Primary School

Emotion Poem (Anger)

Anger is red.
It sounds like thunder
And smells like burning food.
Anger tastes like wicked witches' apples
And looks like a blazing fire.
Anger is going to bed early.

Kerriann Rowe (8)
Avishayes County Primary School

Winter

W oolly hats, long trailing
scarves, all the gloves on
the classroom heater.
I ce-cold snowballs being
hurled across the playground.
N o more football or
playing on the field.
T rainers bringing muddy
sludge into the shivering
classroom.
E mbers sparkling on
the dying fire.
R oast turkey in the
oven for a hot
Christmas meal.

Sophie Lowe (10)
Avishayes County Primary School

Brindle The Rabbit (Haiku)

Brindle the rabbit.
A giant of a rabbit.
Only a baby!

Tom Evans (8)
Avishayes County Primary School

Dying Dolphin In Despair

Trouble in the sea I hear.
Don't know what to do.
The dolphins crying out in pain
There could be something I could do.
Bang. There goes a shotgun.
Another dolphin in despair.
Why kill the beautiful creatures
Gasping for their air?
Then it starts fighting for its life.
The squealing dolphin I can hear.
In a net another dying dolphin
In despair gasping for its air.

Olivia Bale (9)
Avishayes County Primary School

Sunset

As I watch the sun go down
It makes the sky go red and brown.
As I watch the sun go down
It makes me think of light and sound.
As I watch the sun go down
Dreams come floating in my head.
Then I know it's time for bed.

Emily Chant (8)
Avishayes County Primary School

The Dead Fox

Dead fox,
Lying beside the road,
Dead fox,
Run over by cars, vans and trucks.
Nobody cares about the poor,
Dead fox
Lying beside the road,
If we want to keep our foxes,
We must look where we are going,
To keep them alive.

Louis Hill (9)
Avishayes County Primary School

Sadness Is Blue

It sounds like somebody crying
and smells like dead flowers.
Sadness tastes salty
and looks like tears running down
my face.
Sadness is a lonely feeling.

Danielle Steed (8)
Avishayes County Primary School

Bad Luck, Dead Duck

Covered in muck.
Bad luck dead duck.
My eyes have loads of tears,
You'll lie there for years and years.
You had a short life.
That's all you had.
Too bad how sad.
And yet some people are glad.
People like to pick up a gun.
And off they run.
To shoot you
And then the blood peeps through.
Bad luck dead duck.

April Mahoney (9)
Avishayes County Primary School

Emotion Poem (Happiness)

Happiness is pink.
It sounds like angels singing
And smells like roses.
Happiness tastes like Mum's cookies
And looks like the hot sun.
Happiness is opening my presents

Amelia Lowe (8)
Avishayes County Primary School

A Colourful Spring

Yellow daffodils shine in the sun
Blackbirds and robins
Flying in the sky.
Black and yellow bumble bees
Fly from tree to tree to tree.
Dandelions all over the grass
Trying to hide but coming out fast
Buds are popping open for spring
Birds are singing
For me and you.

Keri Jones (9)
Avishayes County Primary School

The Sad Dolphins

People are polluting the sea.
Dolphins are suffering a lot.
Dolphins are dying because of pollution.
Dolphins lying dead.
On the surface of the sea
It is bad.
please *stop.*
Otherwise dolphins will become extinct.

Gemma Facey (9)
Avishayes County Primary School

Boys And Girls Are Just The Same

What's the difference
between a boy and a girl
A boy may have crisp hair
a girl may have beautiful hair.

Boys are just the same as girls. What's the difference?

Boys say well we're better at sport.
But girls have the same abilities.
Boys are just the same as girls. What's the difference?

It's so unfair to girls,
when boys say we're better,
we're really just identical

Boys are just the same as girls. What's the difference?

When girls get home from a hard day's work
What do they do? Wash up, iron, make tea.

Boys are just the same as girls. What's the difference?

When boys get home from a hard day's work
What do they do? Watch TV, read the paper.

Boys are just the same as girls. What's the difference?

How would boys feel if girls
just sat and watched TV.
And boys did all the work.

Boys are just the same as girls. What's the difference?

If a girl went for a job interview, as a surgeon,
and there were more boys,
who would get the job?
Boys of course.

Boys are just the same as girls. What's the difference?

So what do you think?
We feel upset, angry and disgusted.

Boys are just the same as girls. What's the difference?

You decide!

Gemma Lane, Kelly Gunningham, Helen Page
& Jessica Nichol (9-11)
Avishayes County Primary School

Black And White People

Black people, white people
there's just one difference.
Black and white
could make things bright.
It's really not fair, white people
treat black people not as much as themselves
Black and white, please don't fight.
They may feel sad, they may feel lonely.
Black people white people
could make things bright.
May there be a peace.
black and white, please don't fight,
How do you think they feel?
The black people are sad and poor,
upset, angry, and white don't care.
I hope there will be a happiness between them.

Sebastian Martin (11) & Daniel Packer (10)
Avishayes County Primary School

SPRING

Birds sing and start to build nests.
Flowers open and give a sweet smell.
Golden dandelions spread
Like butter over bread.
A sooty blackbird cheeps merrily.
As he sits on a swaying branch.
Baby animals are born
And spring starts over again.

Corinne Cambridge (8)
Avishayes County Primary School

RED FOX, DEAD FOX

Red fox, dead fox,
Save the red fox,
They don't harm us,
So we shouldn't harm them,
Red fox, dead fox,
Save the red fox.

Keith Barge (9)
Avishayes County Primary School

A Frosty Morning

One frosty morning I got out of bed,
I went to my window
And there it was.
It was white and misty, dark and grey.
It looked pretty and was patterned.
It looked like Christmas Day.
The wind was whistling in the trees
Blowing across the floor.
The cars were covered in frost
The grass was icy
And trees were bare.

Leonie Smith (9)
Avishayes County Primary School

Springtime

Assorted daffodils as golden as a crown.
Bees and wasps have yellow pollen filled bodies.
The grass is soft, the bright sun shines on the glittery meadow.
The clouds float through the sky.
Birds feeding their babies.

Katie Lewis (9)
Avishayes County Primary School

DESPERATE DOG

There was a dog
Just walking along
Its fur all in a tangle
It's very thin and bony
I think it is a spaniel

Now there's no dog
Just walking along
It was starving and hungry
He only ate old scraps
Poor thing.

Sophie Plyer (9)
Avishayes County Primary School

THE BEAUTIFUL DOLPHIN

The beautiful dolphin swimming here and there
What a beautiful sight
From over there I wish I could swim with them
In the deep blue sea
They are so beautiful
They are so beautiful I want one of my own.

Michelle Hale (9)
Avishayes County Primary School

My Favourite Things

Getting presents at Christmas is like a treat,
Discos are so neat!
Books are good, because you learn facts,
When you go outside, you'll see some cats!
Going to the beach to hang around,
Playing and jumping on the ground.
Strawberry ice-cream *yum!*
Coming to school to do work,
Playing with my toys,
Riding on my bike,
Playing with my friends,
Roller-skating in my garden.
These are a few of my favourite things.

Zebulon Minett (8)
Catcott County Primary School

Morning Sounds

Toilet flushing
My mum yawning
The crunch of toast
Kettle boiling.
My sister talking
The clink of drinks
And me waking up.

Jessica Huxtable (8)
Catcott County Primary School

Sounds In The Morning

The sun is rising
I'm getting out of bed
The birds are tweeting
And so am I
The car is starting
I'm getting out of the
House
With my bag
I go to school
What a rush.

Jason Haslam (8)
Catcott County Primary School

Springtime

Spring is here
Chicks are hatching
Daffodils and
Daisies are
Out.
The sky is
All blue
And birds sing
Blossom on tree
And you can
Eat ice-cream.

Emily Coombes (7)
Catcott County Primary School

Pins And Needles

Pins and needles prickle and ache,
They fizz and tingle
And go to sleep
They go all stiff and feel numb
In a crowd you'd stand out like a sore thumb.

You stamp up and down
And wiggle your toes
It starts to go
So you keep on jumping
Oh yes it's gone!

Peter Ditchfield (9)
Catcott County Primary School

Pins And Needles

When I sit down too long and cross my legs
I always get pins and needles
And when I stand up it's really
Achy, painful and numb.
I can't lift my leg up because
It's too sleepy, prickly and weird.

Pins and needles is so annoying,
When I put my foot down
And walk on it, it soon goes away.

Amy Dyson (9)
Catcott County Primary School

My Favourite Things

I like football, scoring a goal
And going to Hollywood Bowl,
Eating ice-cream
And having a nice dream,
Playing with a ball and bat
And feeding my cat,
Playing on my computer is very cool . . . especially playing
Mudball Wall,
Going to Splash and going down the tubes,
Having a party - *great!*
Going fishing with my fishing rod,
Playing in the snow,
Going to the fair and winning a big teddy bear!
Christmas Day lots of fun,
And eating a great big bun,
Reading a big book,
Watching horror films,
These are a few of my favourite things.

Daniel Workman (9)
Catcott County Primary School

Pins And Needles

I love pins and needles.
In my hands and feet.
It feels numb then prickly.
Like a hundred needles going into you.
When you have pins and needles,
It's prickly and sharp.

Nicholas Alford (10)
Catcott County Primary School

My Favourite Things

Watching monkeys eating bananas,
Birds flying high in the sky
Dolphins down below in the deep, blue sea,
Lizards that crawl around but never make a sound,
Football is good to score goals and have lots of fun!
Cuddly rabbits that jump a lot,
Drawing cartoons is lots of fun,
Foxes that run fast and hunt a lot,
Playing basketball when the sun is shining bright,
Pancakes because they are yummy in my tummy,
Monsters because they are nice and spooky,
Having a ride on my bike,
These are a few of my favourite things.

Oliver Brown (8)
Catcott County Primary School

Life In The Town

In a town there are,
Many buildings big and small.
Smelly factories giving out smoke,
People rushing home from work.
Traffic roaring through the night
Children playing out of sight.
Lots of glowing, showing shops
Colourful things to make you stop.
Crowded houses, blocks of flats,
Here's the Mayor wearing his hat.

Tom Rigden (9)
Catcott County Primary School

My Favourite Things

Owls going tu-whit tu-whoo in the night,
Cars going *vroom!*
Sharks going swoosh in the water,
My rabbit Twitch munching on the lawn,
Watching TV,
Birdwatching (stalking birds),
I am a good swimmer *splash!* I just dived in!
Cuddling my cats Joe and Blackberry,
Easter eggs sitting on the table,
Hot dogs,
Riding my mountain bike,
Staying down in Cornwall with my aunty.
These are some of my favourite things.

Peter Willcocks (8)
Catcott County Primary School

Bridgwater

Bridgwater is busy,
The river is dirty,
People shopping in the town,
Children shouting,
Grown-ups laughing,
Sedgemoor Splash is full,
With children swimming in the pool,
Traffic lights are stopping you,
Children watch the cinema too.

Alison Baker (9)
Catcott County Primary School

My Favourite Things

Eating a nice juicy apple,
Smelling the blossom on the apple tree,
Hearing ponies trotting,
Cuddling up in bed,
Smelling flowers,
Making things - oh! What fun!
Mrs Hamilton teaching me,
Having a kitten purring,
Nutmeg barking,
My mum and dad calling for me,
The smell of roast dinner,
Licking strawberry ice-cream in the sun,
These are a few of my favourite things.

Kayleigh Warren (9)
Catcott County Primary School

Winter

Hat on
Scarf on
Gloves on.
Look at the snow
All crisp and white.
Time to go outside
For a snowball fight.
Sledging downwards sometimes a fright!
Phew I'm back home asleep at night.

Kathryn Butler (8)
Catcott County Primary School

My Favourite Things

Athletics - running around,
Reading in peace and quiet,
Some yummy chocolate to nibble,
A nice big slice of chocolate fudge cake that melts
in your mouth,
A piece of pizza with melted cheese,
A holiday in the hot sun,
School trips . . . who knows where we'll go next?
Christmas is fun - you're up really early,
Birthday as well, my special day,
Going to discos, dancing all night,
Swimming a lot . . . dive in the water,
The cinema is fun, watch a movie,
These are a few of my favourite things.

Abigail Newe (9)
Catcott County Primary School

Morning Sounds

Dad's tractor's
Brumming.
Sister shouting
To mum.
Toilet flushing.
Cows mooing.
Cereal crunching.
Milking parlour
Starting up.
Please let me have
. . . some sleep!

Stephen Lee (7)
Catcott County Primary School

THE RAIN

It splashes on me.
The cars get wet.
The clouds are grey and dark.
I don't like the clouds.
It makes me feel horrible
And scared.
I wish it could be sunny
Every day.

Katrina Rich (11)
Elmwood School

PETS

Flicka is black and white.
He goes on my bed,
And he goes in the garden.
He is naughty at times,
But I love him lots.

Sian Elizabeth Davies (11)
Elmwood School

SPECIAL DAYS

It's my birthday.
I am happy.
Sarah comes to a party.
We play pass the parcel.

Lisa Palmer (9)
Elmwood School

My Birthday

It's my birthday today,
I had two toys,
The Biker Mice from Mars.
It made me feel happy.
I might have more presents,
But it's a secret.
We're having a surprise.
We have drinks and biscuits,
For all the class.
I am proud on my birthday.

Michael Weeks (10)
Elmwood School

Saturday Morning

Early in the morning
When I'm still yawning
Early in the morning
When the day's still dawning
I open up the curtains, the sky's all clear
I'm glad now 'cos the weekend's here.
No more school and no more work
You should see my face I grin and smirk
At last I can have a lie-in
This time *I* beat the morning . . . I win.

Jake Readman (10)
High Littleton VC Primary School

Darkness

Darkness, darkness all around,
Staring at me all the time,
Darkness all I ever see at night,
Darkness all around.

Darkness, darkness all around,
Noises, noises all I ever hear,
Shadows, shadows everywhere,
Darkness all around.

Darkness, darkness all around,
Silhouettes staring at me,
Darkness I see all the time,
Darkness all around.

Hayley Dando (10)
High Littleton VC Primary School

Feelings About School

When I came to this last class,
I was shy.
I was worried about my work.
But . . .
Now I know, I don't have to worry.

I have to see a special lady,
For my reading and writing,
Now I am feeling good about my
Work . . .
Now I feel fine.

Emma Fellows (10)
High Littleton VC Primary School

SUMMER DAYS

One summer day,
I woke up.
Dogs barking,
People shouting,
Dogs playing,
People play in the parks,
People cheering,
Summer is here.
Play in the summer,
People are happy,
Children play football,
People go on holiday,
Summer is here.

Kelly Dix (11)
High Littleton VC Primary School

PLAYGROUND

People pushing me around,
Children falling on the ground,
Little children laugh and scream,
Whilst the bigger ones sort out their team.

Children playing on the slide,
I expect it's a really good ride,
Other children playing games,
Shouting out children's names,
Suddenly the school bell goes,
All the children line up in rows.

Wayne Honeybun (11)
High Littleton VC Primary School

Colours

Yellow is the colour of the sun,
And the banana that tastes so sweet,
The harvest in the fields gives us
Enough to eat.

Red is the colour of lips so deep,
The colour of sunlight going
To sleep.

Blue is the colour of the sky above,
And the colour of the sea with
The fishes swimming round.

Green is the colour of the grass,
Leaves and trees.
And the colour of the new buds
Blowing in the breeze.

Simone Kidner (11)
High Littleton VC Primary School

The Fox's Colours

Brown is the rough colour of the fox's fur.
The soothing thickness of the fragile tail.

The white chest of the under-belly glistening in the dark night.
Shouting of the crying baby widens the fox's eye.

Black is the colour of its nose, that searches through the rubbish
To see what he can find, scavenging hunting is what he does best.

Yellow is the colour of the star twinkling in the night sky
But you can see them deep in his eye?

Scott Howe (11)
High Littleton VC Primary School

NIGHT'S SECRET

All alone, not in home,
Trailing around in the dark,
Lampposts high up in the sky,
Making the night so bright.

A shiver down my spine trembles in a line,
Making my heart beat faster,
Trees have faces in all of their places
Following footsteps behind me.

Cold sweat running down my neck,
The whistling of the wind,
Standing on a twig can make a loud click,
Out on my own.

A car coming, its light flashing bright,
Foxes scavenging around
So open the door and let yourself in . . .
To night's secret.

Kayleigh Tucker (10)
High Littleton VC Primary School

SPACE

I love staring into the night sky,
Where the moon stands bold and bright,
The stars they gleam like nothing before,
Staring into the night.

The planets stand out just like the moon.
Mercury, Mars and look there's Neptune.
All the different planets just so far away,
I wonder if I could travel and see them one day?

I love staring into the night sky,
Where the sky is becoming bright.
The sun is coming up from its sleep,
Waking up in the light.

Emily May (11)
High Littleton VC Primary School

GHOSTLY FEELINGS

My heart's running wild,
The shiver down my spine,
The footsteps, closer, closer,
Quickly I turn!

The wind's brushing against my face,
I've gone into a cold sweat,
What's that behind me!
It's just a door creaking.

All of a sudden the trees turn into . . .
Oh it's my mind playing tricks on me,
The dogs start howling,
They get louder and louder.
It's almost 12 o'clock,
I feel worse,
Ghostly shapes sweep past my face,
Something scuttles past,
What can it be?

Sasha Cains (10)
High Littleton VC Primary School

What, When, Why?

What makes the world go round,
Why does it spin?

What makes the sun so hot,
Why does it burn?

Who made the dinosaurs,
Why did they die?

What made the fairies,
Why do they fly?

How did God come to be,
Who made you and me?

All these thoughts in my mind,
What, when, why?

Emily Barber (10)
High Littleton VC Primary School

Cartoons

Cartoons, are they real?
Cartoons, are they fake?
Cartoons are they invincible?
I think that's all I can take.
Their funny eyes,
Their funny feet,
You hardly ever see them eat.
They're in some films,
They're on TV,
They're on my wall,
They look at me.

Ross Jones (11)
High Littleton VC Primary School

Colour

Gold is the colour of the sunshine,
Gold glimmers like corn in the field,
Like money to spend,
The fur of a lion's coat,
The glistening of water behind a speeding boat.

Silver is the colour of falling raindrops,
A silver steam train speeding past,
Silver is cold ice.

Black is the colour of the sky at night,
A black cat walking in an alleyway.

Brown is the colour of the fox's coat,
The Victorian town,
The forest and woods.

Nicky Owen (11)
High Littleton VC Primary School

Moving Up Soon

I'm moving up in September but
I don't want to go.
Somervale's a happy school.
I will lose my way
I will miss the coach
Will I make new friends?
Yes I will
No I won't.
Oh please help me find my mind.
I had a letter yesterday
Tells me everything I need to know
Pens, pencils, rubbers, rulers, books, I will lose them I know.

Janine Denning (10)
High Littleton VC Primary School

Food

For breakfast I pour lots of Shreddies in a bowl,
And then pour on lots of milk,
I put on about a spoonful of sugar,
Then I eat it really quick.

For dinner I always have a cheese roll,
With salad cream squirted on top,
I always have a drink of orange squash,
But we're not allowed any pop.

For a snack at four,
I'll have a bag of crisps,
And sometimes a piece of fruit,
I'll have it chopped, sliced cut into bits I'll eat it any old way.

For tea I'll have a big cooked meal,
Like chips and tomato sauce,
Tonight we'll probably have sausages and potatoes and,
That will be our main course.

For pudding we'll have ice-cream or cakes,
Or maybe even gateaux,
On Sundays we always have apple crumble,
But if it's ice-cream it's grumble, grumble, grumble.

Clare May (11)
High Littleton VC Primary School

Jack The Black Cat

Black is the colour of a cat called Jack,
Black is the colour of a funny kind of rat,
The funny kind of rat is sitting on the cat's back.

White is the colour of the silky clouds,
White is the colour of the fluffy snow,
White is the colour of the piece of paper.

Red is the colour of the sweet flavoured strawberry,
Red is the colour of a nice ripe apple,
Red is the colour of bright red blood.

Green is the colour of the grass so long,
Green is the colour of a plant so tall,
Green is the colour of the top of the trees.

Blue is the colour of the top of the sky,
Blue is the colour of the water running by,
Blue is the colour of the cars driving by.

Lauren Willcox (11)
High Littleton VC Primary School

In The Dark

The dark wind's blowing,
Trees are whining,
People shouting,
Dogs barking,
Shadows everywhere,
Owl's hooting to give me a scare.

Donna Heal (11)
High Littleton VC Primary School

The Monster Under My Bed

One night as I crept into bed,
I heard a grunting sound,
What could it be?
A thought came to me,
Maybe it's the bogey monster.

I hide under the cover,
I called for my mother,
But no-one seemed to hear me,
I grabbed my Ted, his name was Fred,
And he began to cheer me.

I pulled myself together,
I sneezed because of a feather
My sheets went flying,
I started crying,
Then my mum came up to calm me.

John Hammond (11)
High Littleton VC Primary School

The Rainbow Fish

Under the sea
Under the sea
you will find a rainbow fish
under the sea
under the sea
you will see a glittering spark
it will zoom straight past you
under the sea
under the deep, deep sea.

James Kingman (8)
Longvernal Primary School

THE RAINBOW FISH

Colourful scales
your fins and your tail shining
glistening pink and blue like
sapphires and emeralds.
You can swim and splash
and even dash.
The little blue fish
came rushing up and said
'Please give to me
one of your beautiful scales.'
'No! No!'
cried the rainbow fish.
No-one was nice to him
but in the end
he gave everyone a scale
and he was happy.

Sarah Moon (8)
Longvernal Primary School

THE WHITE WOLF

When the wolf goes out
Hunters are there, watching out
I hope he will come back
To his family
Every night he goes out
Who would think of hunting him
Oh you'd better watch out, the hunters are about
Leave your home
For some food, but go carefully, the hunters are around.

Michelle Sheppard (9)
Longvernal Primary School

The Rainbow Fish

The rainbow fish was swimming.
He had some silver scales.
The other fish stared jealously.
But he was selfish in the sea.

He shot up and down
the fast rushing sea
He kept on saying 'No!'
to the poor little blue fish
asking for a scale.

'Please,' said the fish
'Oh only one little scale.'
'All right,' he said.

The little fish told
all the other fish.
They came and took a scale
until he had only one scale left.

They were all friends,
'Come on, rainbow fish,'
they shouted.

Andrew Jones (8)
Longvernal Primary School

The Spell Of Evil

Hubble bubble at the double,
Cooking pot stir up some trouble.
Into my pot there must go . . .

An orc's brain boiled,
And a goblin's toe,
Some skeletons' old teeth,
And a snake's tail coiled.

A hobgoblin's sword,
A human's deafening shriek,
A horde of devil ants
And an ear piercing creak.

A muscle of a zombie,
A shell of a snail,
Fresh lava from city Pompeii
And a terrifying scary wail.

Dan Paget (9)
Longvernal Primary School

Weather Riddle

I am a sabre-tooth tiger
In the jungle
I roar as loud as a rocket,
I streak very fast through the sky.
What am I?

Thunder.

Scott Dular (8)
Longvernal Primary School

Super Spell

Hubble bubble at the double
Cooking pot stir up some trouble . . .

Tree trunk skin
and adder's blood.
Boiled in frogs' heads,
with a bear's skin.
Teeth of a wolf,
claws of an eagle,
guts of a seagull.

That's what I need for my
Super spell.
Bang! Oh well.

Daniel Millar (9)
Longvernal Primary School

The Polar Bear

Thick white snow all around
As it falls to the ground
There's something there, fast asleep
One white lump, great big feet
If you get closer up
You won't see one white lump,
You will see a polar bear
Really white fluffy hair
But wait what's in the air
It's a man standing there
With a gun ready to shoot
Better run, use your head
Quick, quick or soon you'll be dead.

Harriet Oliver (10)
Longvernal Primary School

THE WITCH'S SPELL

Hubble bubble let's make double trouble
A frog's head
Let's add a leg.
One or two
A camel's tail
Make it tasty
Mix it well
Let's make it smelly
Let's add a dirty welly
Let's add lemon and wine
And it makes good slime.
Let's add sticks and stones
That will break the people's bones
Now go out get me some hearts
And make some apple tarts.

Zoe Curtis (9)
Longvernal Primary School

WEATHER RIDDLE

I am a fire
colourful and warm
I crackle in the day not dark,
and make you warm.
What am I?

Sun.

Roxanne Watts (9)
Longvernal Primary School

Horses

My favourite animal is the horse,
It's got a beautiful mane and a forelock of course.
They come in different breeds,
They eat grass and sometimes weeds.
They come in many colours and sizes,
My favourite colour is a dark bay.
Horses like apples,
They'd probably like to eat them all day!
At my riding school,
I think it's really cool,
All the horses and ponies,
Never seem to be lonely.
My favourite horse is called Heidi,
She's a pretty dark bay,
And I can control her OK!

Tammy Barrow (11)
Longvernal Primary School

Weather Riddle

I'm like a fire all shiny and bright,
I look down on you from morning to night,
If you come close there will be a sizzle and crack,
Then you'll go home looking all black.
What am I?

The sun.

Andrew Wadley (10)
Longvernal Primary School

Oh Harriet

I have a hamster called Harriet
She's all furry and brown
She plays in her wheel
It makes an awful sound
Creak! Creak! As she goes round and round.

My dad's really fuming
He lets out a shout
'Oh Harriet cut that out!'
So I have to go and get her out
But soon she gets faster and disappears
Down under the sofa.

Now my dad's getting really mad
He tells me to pull the sofa away
So Harriet cannot play
Then I put her away and take her to my room.

That's my hamster Harriet
All furry and brown
Making lots of trouble

But really my hamster is the best
Of the lot.

Rachel Hodges (10)
Longvernal Primary School

THE STORM

Dark clouds glide across the turbulent sky
The heavy rain dives to the ground with a *crash!*
Mothers frantically *zoom!* To get their washing in
People dive, twist, and swirl to get inside
Really it looks like a rugby game and the touch-down's the doorstep.
The game's over now, the doors slam shut
But hats are flying everywhere
Thunder *roars!* With anger
Trees *crash* to the ground, but there is a hope
The sun starts to shine
The storm admits its defeat and moves on.

Graham Bransgrove (11)
Moorlands Junior School

END OF THE WORLD

Sometimes it looks as if it could be,
the end of the world.
When mum and dad scream at you,
when you haven't done anything wrong.
Or when your science project explodes,
when you get a G minus
you feel like blowing the school up.
When your pencil lead snaps again and again.
And when your brother drives you round the bend.
It really could be,
the end of the world . . .

Helen McDonald (11)
Moorlands Junior School

Water Lilies

Water lilies can be white or yellow
Anchored to the bottom of the pond
The flowers and leaves float on the water.
Every night the flowers close and sink
Rising water straightens the stalks.
Leaves grow on glistening long stalks
Insects pollinate the fruit
Lying, floating happily
In the sunlight the fruits are ripe,
Every time the sun is out it sparkles and looks clean
So pretty and beautiful.

Sally Mordaunt (11)
Moorlands Junior School

Outside Always

Outside always is the owl,
Flying up so high,
Below all is resting,
But the owl still flies on,
Swooping soaring in the sky,
Diving on his prey,
A silent bird of the night,
Silently flying on,
I think he's still up there somewhere,
Flying up so high.

Sarah Harwood (10)
Moorlands Junior School

1485 War Poem

Bang! Goes the first bomb!
Bang! Goes the first lot of people!
The doctor shouting for help
Soldiers running to injured people . . .
People rolling in pain . . .
As soldiers die
Bang! Goes the next bomb!
Bang! Goes the next lot of people!
Innocent people getting killed or hurt.
Dead bodies everywhere, more and
More people getting killed
More ladies cry as their husbands die.
As the fighting comes to a stop:
The depressing moment's come.

Sara Shepherd (10)
Moorlands Junior School

Storm In Town

Wind, ripping roofs off houses
Gushing rain down to earth
People running here and there
Twigs zooming everywhere
Telephone cables snapping to bits
Wind howling like a hound
Finally the storm passes on
To the next city beyond.

Jason Duffield (10)
Moorlands Junior School

ALONE

I was alone
I was so lonely
Spooky . . .
There was a knock on the door
I opened the door
There was an old man
He was on the floor
We had no mum or dad
To tell us what to do . . .
Nobody was there
The door bangs . . .
It's gone . . .

Kelly Hinds (10)
Moorlands Junior School

LIVER

One day I was playing on my computer
When mum called 'Teatime.'
'What's for tea?' I asked.
'Liver'
Liver! I hate liver.
'Mum I don't like liver.'
'Well that's for tea.'
'Mum I *don't like liver,*
Can I have a sandwich instead?'
'As long as it's a liver sandwich.'

Luke Stallard (9)
Moorlands Junior School

ALIEN!

No way!
The ship was enormous
It came down with a crash
A creature stepped out
It was big fat and hairy
Its eyes were the size of footballs
I thought it might be a ghoul
But it was way too scary
I ran
And ran
And ran
Until I found somewhere to hide
Then I cried
And cried
And cried
Over above me I saw it again
it was heading to planet Z.

Edward Atkinson (9)
Moorlands Junior School

A LITTLE FISH

He slithers in the stream
And sometimes there's a gleam
From his black beady eye
Watching passers-by.
He's always in a school
So desperate not to die
But someday he will
Oh! Dear little fish I wish I wish . . .

Rosanna Mann (9)
Moorlands Junior School

TEACHERS!

Eyebrows slant
Eyes narrow
Teeth grind
Get in the blue book now!

Reading class book
Somebody whispers
Slams book down
Get in the blue book now!

Boy running down the corridor
Straight into the Head
Head stops him
Get in the blue book now!

Two boys fighting
Teacher walks up
Breaks up the fight
Get in the blue book now!

Ben Butcher (10)
Moorlands Junior School

MY DEVOTED DOG

When I get home from school
My dog quickly runs up the hall
And wants to quickly have a game of football.
Then she licks the ice-cream off my leg.

Gemma Horroll (11)
Moorlands Junior School

My Nanny In Hospital

(This poem is for you)

I can remember when I was little,
and you used to look after me.
We used to play boats on the sofa,
tea party with the dolls.
Play house with the Barbies, bat and ball,
and of course the board games.
Then of course I would have a cup of tea,
in my special cup.

I can remember we used to go down to Moorland Road.
And you used to buy me sweets and things.
So nanny I am looking forward to seeing you home,
So we can go shopping together again.

Rebecca Bath (10)
Moorlands Junior School

My Number Poem

One wet worm walked on a wall.
Two terrible twins talked together.
Three thin thieves thieved three things.
Four fat figs had a fruitful fight.
Five fat flamingos fought for fun.
Six stupid sea serpents swam the sea.
Seven spotted squids swam slowly.
Eight armadillos ate eight amphibians
Nine nutty nits knew nothing.
Ten tubby teddies trumpeted on trombones.

Adrian Clancy (9)
Moorlands Junior School

THE PANTOMIME

Waiting on the stage
The curtain's going back
I'm very, very nervous
There's no looking back.

I'm dancing around
And singing a song
Not looking at the audience
As the music plays on.

Everyone is clapping and cheering
As we curtsy and bow
The curtains go back
To the changing rooms we go

The pantomime has finished
And everyone's going home
I'm very, very tired
So goodbye I'm going home.

Sara King (9)
Moorlands Junior School

A SNOWY MORNING

A snowy morning
all clear and completely white,
covering the plants.

Everywhere is snow
flowers coming from below,
Snowmen in the snow.

Kate Kenny (10)
Moorlands Junior School

Rappin' Friends

We are loud, we are fun,
Listen to our rap because it's just begun.

This is Becky she's always ready,
Keep on rappin' keep it steady,

This is Rachel she is cool
If you mess with her then you're a fool,

This is Kays she knows it all,
She is the highlight of the school,

This is Vicks she's really proud,
With her gym she'll start a crowd,

This is Kath her name's no joke,
She's got the money she's never broke,

Becky and Rach are always right,
Never mess with them or you'll be in a fight,

Kays and Vicks are really good,
They make you feel good like they should,

Now it's down to the last one,
Her name is Kath she's really fun!

Hope you like our rap hope you think it's cool,
Better finish now 'cause it's the end of school.

Becky Winn (10)
Moorlands Junior School

Dad!

Dad is annoyed when he says
'Don't-let-me-hear-you-say-that-again!'
He points his finger at me like a hairy pepperoni,
And shakes it about.
When he is really stressed
He turns psycho,
And lifts me up
By my wrist
and,

W h a c k!

On my bum,
And sends me up to bed.
His hairy pepperoni points to my bedroom door,
Sometimes he shows me up,
And embarrasses me in front of my friends,
By sending me up to my room.

I would love
To do the same
Thing to him!

James Cooper, Greg Avis (9) & Martin James (10)
Moorlands Junior School

The Seal

A head pops out of the heavy layer of silk.
Its rounded head bobs up and down
With eyes that gleam like sapphires.
I thought by the way it looked at me
It had lost its mother in the sea.

Jamie Lorimer (9)
Moorlands Junior School

Spider!

Spider crawling in my bed,
Frightening thoughts come in my head.

The spider crawls onto my arm,
Then snuggles in my lucky charm.

Frightening thoughts come out of my head,
Sadly the spider crawls out of my bed.

Then he goes to pester my sister,
Then there's a sudden cry of :

Spider!

Kayleigh Parkhouse (10)
Moorlands Junior School

Where Will I Go?

I will arise and go to Hollywood
Full of famous people
I will follow the stars if . . .
I could I would maybe I might
bump into someone famous
Big hotels and wedding bells
different people different places!
It isn't the same
Mmm I wonder if it might rain?
I don't know anyone here
I think I might go home.

Laura Preater (10)
Moorlands Junior School

ALIEN BEING

. . . A saucer came
Down from the stars
It has lights all around it
Flashing blue and grey.
A beam
Yellow it was.
It hit the ground
Down it went
Down!
It just about touched me!
I froze in horror
A smoky cloudy alien
With crystallised eyes
Stared at me
Like a valosaraptor
Ready to pounce. I shouted.

Ashdon McFall (10)
Moorlands Junior School

WHEN I AM . . . POEM

When I'm gloomy I feel like rain
When I'm sorry I feel like a popped balloon
When I'm happy I feel like a cheer leader
When I'm lonely I feel afraid
When I'm sleepy I feel like a heavy stone
When I'm bored I feel like a cut-off light.

Alexia Trafford (10)
Moorlands Junior School

The Football Match

A argued with the referee,
B bit a player,
C cried because he missed his mum,
D dribbled down the wing,
E got excited over nothing,
F fouled a player,
G got a red card,
H hogged the ball,
I got injured,
J jumped for a head,
K kicked the ground with rage,
L liked football,
M mugged the linesman,
N was (k)nackered,
O opened his half-time snack,
P puked up on the pitch
Q quit
R ran,
S scored a goal,
T tackled a player,
U unlocked the changing room door,
V vandalised the net,
W whacked the ball,
X had an x-ray on his leg because he broke it,
Y yawned
Z zoomed down the wing.

Oliver Rose (10)
Moorlands Junior School

Smelly Trainers

For years I've had my trainers,
They've kept my tootsies warm,
Through snow they've trudged,
Through mud they've squelched,
Kept me dry in a storm,

My trainers have ridden my bike,
And also my Teeny Tots trike,
My trainers have been to Sainsbury's shopping,
And upon my horse a trot-trotting.

My trainers go everywhere with me,
They've shrunk in the wash,
They've climbed my tree.

But now they're old and scruffy,
The laces are frayed too,
There is just one thing I need to say,
I think their life is through.

Kathryn Bishop (10)
Moorlands Junior School

Henry VIII

Henry VIII, a very fat man
Wouldn't do you a favour even if he can
Catherine of Aragon was his first wife
And he made her lose her life
When he became like a pope
He thought he was a bit of a dope
Although he was a Catholic
He didn't know which wife to pick.

Laura West (10)
Moorlands Junior School

A Stormy Night

It is a stormy night,
You could even fly a kite,
It's so windy,
Electricity out,
Mother gives a shout,
Night has fallen,
Trees blown over,
Tiles off roofs,
People inside,
No-one out,
Shops all closed,
Cockerel on church turned to south,
Leaves twist off trees,
The wind howls around the town,
Branches tumble to the ground,
One lady bangs her door shut,
Her umbrella is inside out,
Morning is rising,
All is quiet.

Ann-Elyse Hector (10)
Moorlands Junior School

My Hamster

My hamster doesn't sleep at night
He sleeps in the day when it is light,
He runs in his wheel faster and faster
And then has some food and drink after.
I don't know why he sleeps in the day
But I love him anyway.

Erin Conlon (10)
Moorlands Junior School

WINTER

Glistening silver under a dark bleak sky,
Frosty, gloomy, black clouds sailing by.
The icy smooth snow - the creepy black wood,
The stream does not flow, I roll in the mud.
Slush! Mush! Crunch on dead leaves,
My fingers are numb, my toes are froze,
To think in summer I was under a hose!
The scene is dazzling, very bright,
even though it's not at all light.
The dead looking trees are completely white
It might be almost, nearly night.
My nose is red, I'm as stiff as lead,
But still I don't want to go to bed.
Slip, slide, slide and glide,
All the animals have gone to hide!
Why does winter come once a year?
Sometimes I hate feeling spring's very near!

Madeleine Patston (10)
Moorlands Junior School

HOW TO MAKE A SPIDER

She needs . . .
Eight legs like pipe cleaners . . .
All those eyes blinking at you like flashing lights . . .
Deadly venom squirting at you like a water pistol
Hiding in your rubbish bin like a bit of potato peel
Spinning their webs like a construction site
And lurking in corners like a grain of dust.

Edward Beeching (11)
Moorlands Junior School

Winter

Cold short days,
Long frosty nights,
No bright sun but misty clouds,
Icy taps and frosty water,
A thick quilt wrapping around me,
My pillow with an inch of crunchy snow,
The snow is getting deeper and deeper,
My chilly feet in hot bubbly water,
My mouth is cracking open,
My cold frozen nose is getting sore,
My little hands are frozen to bits,
I'm as cold as an ice-cube,
We're all falling over on the slippery ice,
Frosty roads with cars all over the place.

Katrina Ashton (10)
Moorlands Junior School

Winter

Short dark days,
Skiddy wet icy roads,
Frozen feet dead in a bin,
A blanket of crunchy snow,
A white rabbit with a frozen tail,
Cold hands and messed-up hair,
Misty windows and chilly feet,
Frosty taps and frozen water,
Dead cold fish on a little lilypad
Slippery ice in the sea,
In a hot bath fast asleep.

Jennifer Avis (11)
Moorlands Junior School

WINTER

As you walk across the grass, crunch under your feet.
Cold winter's air flies everywhere.
Leaves crunchy, icy and cold.
A snowman chilling in the breeze.
Fluffy white snow like cotton wool blowing all around.
Cold and icy winds.
Fingers are as cold as winter.
The streets are deserted.
Cattle's warm breath blowing in the wind,
You need to use hats, scarves and gloves.
Frost swooping on the grass.
Winter
The last season of the year . . .

Kimberley Gingell (10)
Moorlands Junior School

WINTER

Winter streets covered in snow,
Children wearing lots of clothes,
Parents drinking cups of tea,
Children cuddling their teddy bears tight,
Children huddled up in bed all night,
Children shouting 'Snowball fight!'
Mothers shouting to give them a fright,
Snowballs travelling fast through the air,
Winter jumpers being taken out of drawers,
Summer dresses hanging in the wardrobe,
Families sitting in a lovely warm house,
Frost biting like a burning fire,
Winter's here at last!

Keri Lewis (11)
Moorlands Junior School

PAINTING THE TOWN WHITE

A big cold icy man was painting
the town white.
Children in their beds all night
dreaming of snow
all crisp and white . . .
Winter creeps into your mind
leaving autumn behind.
City streets all covered in snow
hoping that it will soon go.
Owls in their feathers like a doll in its lace.
Dogs running like Sports Day in a race.
The man has finished painting the town
white.

Carley Robson (11)
Moorlands Junior School

FLYING

I Speedwell the pigeon,
Swooping
low through the sky.
When gliding high, high above the clouds,
Like a flying butterfly.
I Speedwell in a race.
The starter goes 1, 2, 3.
I flap my wings as hard as hard
And swoop low to home.
Next day I swoop up,.to the tree above,
And perch my feathers
On a branch.

Samantha Edson (11)
Moorlands Junior School

The Battle (Bosworth Field)

The drums boom out the war cry,
The men rush and meet,
Clash! Bang! Go the swords,
The shields block the thrusts,
The musket men stand and fire,
Boom . . . crash . . . boom,
The bullets fall like killer rain,
The cries of men in their death throes,
The arrows fly straight and true,
Many a man dies too soon,
For their young lives . . .
The men are loyal,
They'll die for their King,
Many do . . .
But they keep on fighting,
Not caring about their wounds,
The King shoots down towards good Henry,
Slicing at him with his sword,
But the King is dragged down,
Slaughtered,
The battle is won!
Hooray! Hooray!
But not without cost . . .
Many a man died on this day . . .
But the battle is won,
Dead bodies lie on the field,
Richard is dead,
Henry is King . . .
Crowned on this day,
After this day,
Everyone remembers the battle . . .
The battle . . .

Joe Clacey (11)
Moorlands Junior School

WINTER

A fast and furious snowball fight,
In the school grounds.
Father Christmas stuck down our chimney,
I'll get him a pie!
Crackers exploding,
And bursting with joy.
Presents.
Standing at about 10 metres high,
Robins perched on a branch,
Singing their merry song . . .
Bare trees that look like skeletons
In the snow . . .

Craig Herman (11)
Moorlands Junior School

BOOKS

Books are happy sometimes sad,
without books we wouldn't be glad.
We wouldn't be able to read for a start
and that would really break our hearts.
We learn from books old and new.
Without books what would we do?
How would my head feed information
to my brain?
How would I put my pen to paper again.
Books are here to stay forever
Without book I don't think so, never.

Louise Fullrook (11)
Moorlands Junior School

WINTER

The snowballs on the garden shed,
The sledges down the hill,
All shops with lights and decorations,
The snow is raining down,
The gritter on the roads still,
After a long and dangerous night.
The ice skates out, and ready to wear,
Then all around the pond!
Then back inside,
The fire, it's burning big and bright,
The carols ringing through the streets,
The meat is in the oven,
The present sitting by the tree,
The star is on the top.
Last night the stockings
Hanging by our beds
And now they're filled with presents.

Daniel Rich (11)
Moorlands Junior School

ALL ALONE

All alone in the dark
What's that! I hear something
Help someone!
Look, shadows getting closer
Oh no! The lights have gone off
Help they're getting closer
The light's on again
But they're still there
Oh no! The light has gone off!

Emma Escott (11)
Moorlands Junior School

WINTER

The trees are bare with waving fingers,
Grass crackling with ice.
The flies won't be fooled,
Webs are clear,
Snow is sparkling white.
Footprints embedded in the ground.
Crunch, crack, crunch, is the only sound.
The road is covered with a fluffy duvet,
The sliding sledges are coming my way.
Frost-bitten fingers, a red runny nose,
Crunchy ice covering the curled up hose.
The winter wind sweeps coats around,
Slush and snow is on the ground.
The air is sharp,
The mist is thick . . .
Warm clothes and woollen gloves.
Robins trill from their frosty perch.
The winter is cold.
Freezing.

Carla Pedwell (11)
Moorlands Junior School

HAVE YOU EVER WONDERED?

Have you ever wondered
Why the sky is blue?
Why the sun is round?
And why the cows go *moo?*

Have you ever wondered
Why the grass is green?
Why the moon at night
Is the brightest ever seen?

Where can I find the answers
To these questions that we have?
I know what I'll do,
I'll go and ask my dad.

Natalie Hudson (10)
Moorlands Junior School

Sailing, Soaring . . .

The pigeon sails over fields,
Spreading his wings over the land,
Gliding and swooping,
Diving and looping in the clear,
Blue sky,
High up in the air,
Flapping wings,
Small people down below,
Like a swarm of tiny bees,
Gliding like a butterfly,
Feathers grey and white,
Soaring the skies,
Beating his long,
Long,
Wings,
Right to the tip of the wings,
People waving up to them,
Watching them swoop like eagles.

Lindsay Robinson (11)
Moorlands Junior School

WINTER

Icy wind bellowing through the rafters.
Crunchy leaves crunching under my feet.
Leafless trees surrounding you.
Slidy ice on paths everywhere.
Cold nights closing in.
Light fading away . . .
Clouds isolating you from the blue sky.
Feet frozen in the frosty grass.
Slipping on ice on the way to school.
Winter is like a lion ready to pounce!
Snowflakes falling from the sky.
Darkness closing in on you.
Autumn fading away into the darkness . . .

Tommy Freeman (11)
Moorlands Junior School

WINTER

Bare trees looking like skeletons,
Eerie winds in the nights,
On Boxing Day there are snowball fights,
Sledge races with ramps too,
Snow on the ground, sticking like glue,
Snow on the houses like icing on a cake,
Floating ice glaciers on the pond surface,
Snowmen in the fields,
Looking like scarecrows . . .
A warm Christmas dinner,
Sitting on the dining room table,
Snow hitting our roofs,
Like Santa Claus and his reindeer.

Robert Mould (11)
Moorlands Junior School

WATER SCORPION

With its long hairs so as not to get wet
And its prey-catching forelegs
Tiny creatures live in fear of them
Eggs are laid on plants
Resting in wait for anything to eat.

Size does not matter
Catching all the prey
Only a tail to breathe through
Reaching higher speeds than anything else
Powerful wings alert
Insect of the water
On and under the pond
Never a victim.

Graham Dorey (11)
Moorlands Junior School

WINTER SNOW

There are snowflakes falling from the sky,
Snowball fights in the fields.
The snow shining in my eyes.
White frost on the windows.
The ground as white as a polar bear.
A snowman as big as me.
Christmas is here and the town is busy.
Small animals gathering food.
I look like Rudolf the red nosed reindeer.
The whole town is white, a spark of green
shows in the trees.

Kim Griffin (10)
Moorlands Junior School

NEWCOMERS

My father came to England
From another country
Far far away.

He brought me many gifts
We played many games
We read beautiful stories
And he tucked me into bed.

But when morning comes
We play our favourite games
We also play sports.

I love weekend
When I can play with my Dad

When he tucks me into bed
Our last words to each other are

Goodnight, goodnight!

Vicky Kirk (10)
Moorlands Junior School

THE CHRISTMAS STORY

(From the point of view of Mary)

I was in the field this morning picking crops for tea
for Joseph and me,
When just then a big light was behind me,
I turned around and said 'Cor blimey!'
I saw an angel that was bright,
Her name Gabriel, what a sight,
She said something I couldn't hear,
The word 'baby' caught my ear.
I jumped for joy now Joseph had come,
I told him the news and he stuck up his thumb.
The next day we had to go to Bethlehem,
To the place where we were born,
But there was no inn for us to stay in,
So we had to search all day,
Until we found an inn for us to stay.
So then I had a baby boy,
A crib is where he lay.
The little baby that giggled was going to be the
King some day,
Then three men came,
Wise were they,
They gave my baby three gifts,
And said 'Here are three gifts for you,'
'I hope you like them they're all for you'
said another.
As they went the sheep went '*Baaaa'*
and the cows went *'Moooo!'* we settled
down and said 'Toodle loo!'

Kerry McLeod (11)
Moorlands Junior School

WINTER

Snowball fights with exploding bombs,
Eerie winds whistle and howl.
Skeleton trees.
Misty moonlight shimmers in the breeze,
Snow on houses like icing on a cake,
Snowmen being beheaded by the icy wind.
A brown plucked turkey roosts on the plate,
Open the many doors see the many scenes
Eat the milky chocolate.
A blitz of cards and presents,
Sledge racers, ramming and shoving,
Red noses,
Whiter than white,
Snow on the ground.

James Land (11)
Moorlands Junior School

DREAM BIRD

I woke up this morning.
I heard a noise like singing.
A pigeon outside my window . . .
I shut my eyes and imagined . . .
Me, a pigeon . . .
Flying, gliding and soaring.
Looping around the sky,
Looking down at Toy Town.
I would win all races.
I, a champion!
Stop dreaming!
I'm not a pigeon!

Olivia Turner (11)
Moorlands Junior School

Jumping Frog

Jumping frog,
Under the water
Munching up all the flies,
Picking its step carefully,
In the weed it lies,
Nothing can turn it away
from the pond,
Grass snakes can sometimes.
Finally it is night-time,
Running and hopping to shelter,
Out in the dark the foxes come,
Good to be hidden away!

Ffion Hughes (10)
Moorlands Junior School

The Hunted Horse

I walked outside,
there he was.
His dense black body
showed up like charcoal against
the sparkling white snow
cantering furiously
jumping, trying to get out
bucking hard
open the gate
into the woods
free!

David Ellis (10)
Norton-Sub-Hamdon C of E Primary School

My Sea Horse

Up, up, up he comes,
Galloping forward and up,
Tiny hooves like two little thumbs,
With an almighty buck.

The white wave sea horse,
That's him, yes,
At his best,
With his mane, all coarse.
His lovely white tail now showing.

Waves come over,
His pretty white head, in all its glory,
Turning back, back again,
White hooves in the air.

Galloping, galloping, galloping now,
Across the beach he goes.

Down, down, down,
To the depths,
Out of sight, he vanishes.
Bubbles, bubbles, lots of bubbles,
Out of sight he vanishes.
I wonder if I'll ever see him again?
Out of sight he vanishes.

Going down,
Deeper, deeper,
Out of sight, he vanishes.
Going, going,
Gone.
Forever!

Emily Tavernor (9)
Norton-Sub-Hamdon C of E Primary School

MY WEEKEND ON THE FARM

I wake up in my cosy snug and warm bed.
I feel the breeze coming in the window.
I get out of bed.
I feel like I have just come back from the dead.
I play with my AFX.
Now I am charging down the stairs.
Past some chairs.
I open the old rattly door.
To our warm old kitchen.
I get out my breakfast and get it down my
Neck fast.
I walk to the powerful truck through some muck.
I get in the back with our dog.
I like today, let's load up some hay.
Then off we go to feed some sheep.
We will start a new day.

Andrew Tavernor (9)
Norton-Sub-Hamdon C of E Primary School

ANIMALS

The fluffy white rabbit
Chews on the lettuce,
The golden soft guinea pig
Hides under his warm straw bed,
The green scaly frog likes to hop
Onto lily pads which float on the water,
The galloping horse rides with his owner
It likes eating oats and grass,
And all the humans like to do is . . .
Watch TV with the newspaper - what a waste!

Stuart Burridge (10)
Norton-Sub-Hamdon C of E Primary School

Once On A White Winter's Night

On a white winter's night a
creaking is heard, opening the door
creeping up the stairs.

Now on the landing no footsteps
to be heard . . . windows
blow open *whoosh* go the curtains,
lantern goes swinging,
falling down, screaming is heard
a white figure is seen . . .

but that is all
or is it?

Thomas Sams (9)
Norton-Sub-Hamdon C of E Primary School

The Dolphin

Once I went out
on a sea trip
fishing
I caught
mackerel, cod and herring.
It was late when I got back to the harbour
the fishermen were . . .
killing a dolphin!
But now I can thankfully watch dolphins roam free
splashing, swiftly through the water
jumping, leaping fast but calm.

Jamie Rees (9)
Norton-Sub-Hamdon C of E Primary School

THE GLOOMY SCHOOL

My mum couldn't wait till I
went back to school.
To write read and play.
My friends said that school is
OK
To laugh and enjoy yourself
and have lots of fun.
It's the day I am moving in.
'Have a good day.'
I move against the foggy hills
and walk against the trees.
'What a wonderful gloomy
school.'
I think I'll like it here
Ha ha ha ha ha.

Natasha King (10)
Norton-Sub-Hamdon C of E Primary School

GREEN EYES

I was starting to get ready for bed.
I brushed my teeth and brushed my hair.
I looked around there was something there.
He was black, I turned on the light he was
gone with the flick of the light.
I got into bed. I remember what he looked like.
I said he had big black green eyes
He looked right at me, and then he ran
and then I looked outside.
It was only a cat because you know
cats' eyes are bright and you can see them clearly.

Charlote Fallows (10)
Norton-Sub-Hamdon C of E Primary School

Playing At Wembley

It's always been my dream,
playing at Wembley.
All the top stars go there,
but never ever me.
I ask Mum to let me go but she always says
No!
Why?
Too much money!
Huh!
Seven weeks passed and still no luck
of going to play at Wembley.
Tut!
Tut!
Two days later when hope was nearly gone
a postcard came from London.
It's addressed to me with football
stickers on!
I rip it open faster than you can say
Jack Robinson!
Yes!
At last!
I'm going to play at Wembley!

Mark Wiggins (9)
Norton-Sub-Hamdon C of E Primary School

Feelings

The treasures of you being my mum
And the treasures of you being the best of friends
Is enough to cover Easter or my birthday
But most of all my heart.

Philippa (10)
Norton-Sub-Hamdon C of E Primary School

The School Holidays

My mum could not wait until I got back
to school.
She got fed up with me saying
I've got nothing to do.
If I was back to school,
            I could
                        Write
                        Read
                        Play
                        Talk
                        Draw
And then learn something new each day
At last the holidays have ended.

Emily Davis (9)
Norton-Sub-Hamdon C of E Primary School

Skiing

Gliding through the snow on two, long skis,
Is quite exhilarating with knocking knees,
With the wind in your face,
And the wind behind your back,
You really go fast without a backpack.
You go up a lift and cling on tight,
And when you get to the top you have a good sight
A confident skier skims and glides down the slope,
His name is Tom Watts.
Important people come and see me ski,
They don't know how I can cope!
They think I look so fine,
I can't believe I'm only nine!

Tom Watts (9)
Norton-Sub-Hamdon C of E Primary School

The Mysterious Animal

Ahhh
A gleaming sun on a dazzling cliff edge
Looking down on the calm shining sea
But what's that?
Shuffling through those rather harsh looking
gorse bushes,
There again climbing up that
scarred ash tree,
What is it?
What is it, I say
I think I'd better investigate,
but first I need some protection
hmmm . . . this wet salty driftwood will do,
Now to go and find out what
this thing is.
Better step quickly and carefully,
Not a stir is happening, too quiet for me,
What's that noise?
A sort of 'kuk kuk kuk', noise,
There up there what is it?
It's a, it's a . . .
It's a brown furry bushy tailed
Squirrel!
All that for nothing.

Robbie Milton (9)
Norton-Sub-Hamdon C of E Primary School

THE TIGERS

The fierce tiger leaping through the jungle
Exhausted, thirsty creature.
Green lush leaves rustling on his body.
He stops he notices me.
I come closer and stare into his bright,
bold, frantic eyes,
He pounces
He roars with a frantic bite
Claws as sharp as knives,
Then he turns away like he hasn't seen
me there.
Swishes his tail, it's like he has noticed
something else
I am frozen to the spot
Terrified.

Hannah Peck (10)
Norton-Sub-Hamdon C of E Primary School

THE LION

The fierce scary lion,
With a long swishy tail and large glaring eyes.
The king of the beasts pouncing on its prey.
His long, dirty, shaggy mane swaying from side to side.
He lives in a cave in the middle of the jungle ready to
jump into action,
His ripping teeth and gigantic claws ready to tear into
anything.
Then he stares at his prey,
He crouches down in the long swaying grasses and waits
to pounce.

Amie Calder (10)
Norton-Sub-Hamdon C of E Primary School

When I Was Two

When I was two I had a cot,
A big wooden cot with stickers on it,
I loved my cot,
It made me feel safe,
When I couldn't sleep,
I watched my mobile go round and round,
Then one day my daddy said,
'It's time you had a big bed,'
I didn't like this idea,
So I screamed right into Daddy's ear,
'Don't worry my dear I'll always be here,'
My daddy said,
And that night I slept in my big bed.

Claire Brown (10)
Norton-Sub-Hamdon C of E Primary School

Stormy Day

I wake up in the morning,
I look out of my window,
The sky hangs low, gloomy and grey,
Then it comes, the rain,
Dripping down the gutter,
I get dressed
Go down stairs,
The house is dark, it's a gloomy day,
I switch on the light,
Then smash crash bash!
The lightning comes,
The storm has started.

Hannah Venn (9)
Norton-Sub-Hamdon C of E Primary School

BUGS

I caught a worm in the garden,
It was very long and wiggly.
I showed it to my brother but he just squealed.
I thought boys were supposed to be brave.
It seems some people are scared of worms.
That does not bother me.
I named my worm Beano.
Then I went to have my tea.
In the shed there was a snail.
I showed my dad and he went pale.
I'd put it there the day before.
I like snails.
Earwigs do not pinch.
Some people think they do,
It's just a lot of nonsense.
Some people have nightmares about bugs.
They think I'm round the twist.
Girls think bugs are gory.
They think that they are silly.
Adults think bugs are a nuisance
And worms just make the garden good.
Some think they are scary
To me they're different.

Holly Edmond (9)
Norton-Sub-Hamdon C of E Primary School

My Brother

Can't do it,
Won't do it,
That's what he says.
Can't do it,
Won't do it,
And he stomps off to his bed.
Can't do it,
Won't do it,
And I'm staying here he says.
And look what we done for him.

Rachel Holloway (9)
Norton-Sub-Hamdon C of E Primary School

Silence

Silence is when you hear things.
Listen . . .
The swaying of the grass
Bees buzzing around a buttercup
A caterpillar's feet tip-tapping on a leaf.

Silence is when you hear things.
Listen . . .
A snowflake falling slowly
The wind swifting through the trees
A snowball snuggling down on the soft snow.

Silence is when you hear things.
Listen . . . listen . . .

Leah Byrne (8)
St Gildas RC Primary School

Sunlight

Sunbeams, beaming down
Faint shadows appear on the ground
A powerful source.

John Ellery (9)
St Gildas RC Primary School

Silence

Silence is when you hear things.
Listen . . .
The swaying of the fish's fins,
The shifting of the clouds,
The ascension of the sun.
Silence is when you hear things.
Listen.

Christopher Dutch (8)
St Gildas RC Primary School

Lightning

Bright lightning flashes
Zig zag patterns in the sky
Cutting night in half.

Hollie Linscott (9)
St Gildas RC Primary School

STAR

Tiny dot of light
Making its way through the night
Very carefully.

Holly Fischer (9)
St Gildas RC Primary School

RAINBOWS AND CRYSTALS

Crystals make rainbows
When it is a sunny day
White light becomes colour.

Kristian Parsons (9)
St Gildas RC Primary School

THE SUN

Hot and fiery
The sun gives off light
It's made of fire.

Daniel Brown (9)
St Gildas RC Primary School

STARS

A tiny light dot
A brilliant speck of light
Stars are really bright.

Adam Walmsley (8)
St Gildas RC Primary School

HEAT

The scorching of heat
As the strong sun bursts with light
No shade to be found.

Charlotte Osborne (9)
St Gildas RC Primary School

STARS

Eyes in the night sky
Stars looking down from above
Nature's own torch light.

Robert Brolly (8)
St Gildas RC Primary School

First Light

Light shines through dimness
Brings a cheerful smile to earth
Won't let darkness through.

Cara Hodkinson (9)
St Gildas RC Primary School

Light

The sun is a star
The sun shines through the window
The sun is our light.

Richard Godden (9)
St Gildas RC Primary School

The Sun

How on earth can all
That energy be held in
The strong white hot sun?

Matthew Last (9)
St Gildas RC Primary School

LIGHTNING

Lightning flashes bright
Cutting zigzags through the sky
Power to make fire.

Jason Hinkins (8)
St Gildas RC Primary School

THE SUN

The sun is so hot
It is more hot than lava
Heat that's blistering.

Jessica Fry (8)
St Gildas RC Primary School

TAKING TURNS

Darkness takes the light
So that it can have its rest
Returning brighter.

Danielle Ward (9)
St Gildas RC Primary School

Stars

Stars gleam in the sky
They flash like a bolt of light
Stars high in the sky.

Mark Hinkins (8)
St Gildas RC Primary School

Stars

Light beams travelling
The flickering of a torch
Stars in the night-time.

Luke Gordon (9)
St Gildas RC Primary School

The Rainbow

Rainbow has colour
A bright stripe in a dull sky
Made by rain and sun.

Danielle Critchley (8)
St Gildas RC Primary School

THE MOON

A white round night light
Glowing in the midnight sky
Until the dawn comes.

Rebecca Jeffery (8)
St Gildas RC Primary School

STARS

The sparkling shine of
Glowing stars that fill the sky
To lead the way home.

Martin Mitchell (8)
St Gildas RC Primary School

THE MOON

It's dark on the moon
And there is no gravity
Anything can float.

Nicholas Withers (9)
St Gildas RC Primary School

Star

In this dark, dark night
A single star guides you home
Does it feel lonely?

Phoebe Savidge (8)
St Gildas RC Primary School

Night

The sun is sleeping
The moon is in charge tonight
Stars twinkle with glee.

Natasha Wood (9)
St Gildas RC Primary School

Stars

Shining in the night
Like a torch's tiny beam
Guiding the way home.

Mareez Farag (9)
St Gildas RC Primary School

Sunset

I watch the sunset
Fire glow of vivid colour
Orange, yellow, red.

Amanda Maddalena (9)
St Gildas RC Primary School

Oh Brother!

I bet you've heard such a thing
That brothers are annoying
They push, pull, fight and scream
And blame you for everything
They won't give up without a doubt
Even if you shout!

I hope you've learnt a lesson from my talking
That brothers are a pain
They want you to do everything
But don't I tell you, don't.
They'll tell you again and again
Even if you won't
So take my advice and
Don't get a brother!

Natalie Hulford (10)
St Mary's C of EVC Primary School

The Places My Dad Could Work

The place my dad could do his work,
In France and Egypt and Alberqurq.
Nigeria, the Bahamas and Algeria too,
Australia, America and Timbuktu!
In capital cities like Berlin and Rome!
But no he lives in his study because he
Works at home.

Stephanie Pow (10)
St Mary's C of EVC Primary School

There Was An Old Woman

There was an old woman from Knotty,
Who was completely dotty,
But she also was so true,
That her hands turned blue,
And her face turned even more grotty.

Christine Cooper (11)
St Mary's C of EVC Primary School

Tomb

T ombstones are cold, dirty and
O ld
M ummies are
B uried as they grow old.

Lauren Tranter (10)
St Mary's C of EVC Primary School

A Lie In Bed

No-one to bother me
No-one at all
Just Mum coming upstairs
All droopy and dull

She opens the curtains
To let in the light
I open my eyes
And see such a sight

I turn on the TV
And stay in bed
I feel ill
Something's hammering on
My head.

Chloe Hebden (11)
St Mary's C of EVC Primary School

My Relatives

My relatives Bill and Ted,
Auntie Flo and Uncle Fred,
Grandma Rose and Grampa Bert,
Cousin Lauren and cousin Kurt,
Auntie Sue and Uncle Mark,
Kate and David, Mr Lark,
Second cousins Marg and Conny,
My cousins Faye, Louise and Johnny,
Some of them drive me mad,
But as they love me I'm really glad.

Katherine North (10)
St Mary's C of EVC Primary School

War

I sit here in my chair
Remembering the war.
Bombs hit the ground.
Exploding into flames.
Mines hidden
Shotguns shooting
That's what the war was about.

Muddy fields where poppies lie
Waiting, to come up
Too scared to grow
There is misery everywhere.
People killed, death has struck.
That's what the war was about.

People killing
People dying
There was hope of survival
Why was there killing
Why were there bombs
People losing families.
That's what the war was about.

Emily Shannon (10)
St John's RC Primary School

Moving

A big empty room,
Lies still beneath me.
And the howling of the wind,
Spreads across the floor.
Leaves scatter around my
Feet.
My old house to which I,
Said goodbye.
Gives me a million,
Wonders which sink inside.
To what has happened,
And why? Why?
Why?
The empty room is boring,
And plain.
But how I wish,
I was in my old house,
Again.

Maureen Indoe (11)
St John's RC Primary School

Thoughts

I am laying in my bed, the pillow is so
Comfy under my head.
The stars are so bright, it seems so right,
That they shine in God's sky at night.

Kieren Davies (8)
St John's RC Primary School

ALLIGATOR

Deep low in the murky waters,
in a swamp in the everglades,
An alligator looks around,
and tries to find some prey.
He wanted something to eat,
to turn it into meat.
My teeth you see,
shine and glee.
I smile as I see,
my dinner luxury.
My long tail, is my propeller,
but look over there a tiny fella.
He's going to die.
please don't cry.
Come closer, my friend,
I won't pretend.
I go fast,
I've got you at last.

Hannah Wiltshire (11)
St John's RC Primary School

TOUCAN

So colourful in the jungle
So swift in the air
Such marvellous colours
A fantastic sight
Such beauty in the jungle
Such beauty in the air
How can such beauty be created from an egg.

Kieran O'Neill (11)
St John's RC Primary School

The Sun

It rises in early dew
Cold and damp
The wind whistles and whips
Through the trees
Silence
I listen
Silence
Falling from the sky
The first raindrop
Breaks the silence
Another after another
Clouds hide the sun's bright face
Waiting, it stops
The sun shows its sunny face again
All through the day.

Danielle Hartrey (10)
St John's RC Primary School

Horse

The beat of hooves fills the air,
A black mane,
and brown gleaming fur,
He stops and rears
up to the moon,
Fighting noisily up the mountain path,
gets up to the top and stop,
Mane blowing in the night wind.
King.

Antonia Forsyth (11)
St John's RC Primary School

Bun

It's in my sight lying there.
It's soft and tender.
It makes an aroma, yummy
and nutritious.
It makes a lovely noise, while
it's cooking crispy and brown.
I bite a piece out of it, it's
luxurious - it's crispy and brown.
I take another bite, it's better than
the first one.
It's still got that aroma.
It's still soft and tender.
I take another bite, boy does that
taste good.
I can hear it calling to me, to just
pick it up and eat it.
I take another bite, a big big bite
a bite so big, I've eaten all that
was left - it's gone.
Yum.

Paul Lockett-Wilson (11)
St John's RC Primary School

The Sun And Rain

How moist the spring grass,
Scattering dryness and soil.
Then came the warm sun.

Sam White (9)
St John's RC Primary School

Black Widow

Blow with me,
Flow with me.
Fill my heart with your desire,
You know my love is a burning fire.

My darling is not good enough for me,
Which makes my face fill up with glee.
He will have to be my prey,
He won't live another day.

First his arm,
To do him harm.
Second his tiny little head,
Then goodbye, you are dead.

Teresa Ashman (11)
St John's RC Primary School

Colours

Blue is the sea, the sky
Yellow is the sun, the sand
Red is the blood
Pink are our faces
Orange is hot
Black is night
White is bright
Brown is chocolate
Purple is the sunset

I love all colours
Of the rainbow.

Sian Brady (10)
St John's RC Primary School

THE LION

The lion opens his wide mouth,
and shows his sharp and fearsome teeth.
Then he closes it.
Maybe he's waiting to be fed,
or maybe he's waiting for his freedom
in the wild.

The lion looks powerful and fierce,
when he yawns he looks as if he's going
to bite.
When he's asleep he looks as if he's
going to pounce.

The lion would be happy if he was free
to roam in the wild.
But he is locked up in the zoo.
I think he should be set free,
don't you?

Sarah Hoy (10)
St John's RC Primary School

NIGHT CATS

Black cats
are night cats
they come out in the night
have green eyes like balls
have big black ears.
Their tails are black all over
so if they come out,
don't be afraid.

Sally Sutton (10)
St John's RC Primary School

MIDNIGHT THOUGHTS

Midnight,
The end of yesterday or
The beginning of tomorrow
Who knows?
Not I.
But I have seen wonders
A moonlit lake,
Warm summer nights,
When even the birds can't bear
To sleep.
Frosty, bitter nights,
Where the icicles clothe the
Hedges and fields.
Cool, fresh, spring nights,
Where, as if out of nowhere,
Rain droplets tumble down, down
Making ripples in the water.
Breathless, thundery nights,
When the sky is lit with
Bolts of lightning.
And bleak wintry nights,
When the snow blankets
The ground.
All these things I see,
As a cat.
Midnight,
The end of yesterday or
The beginning of tomorrow
Who knows?
Dong.

Harriet Pope (11)
St John's RC Primary School

The Tree

The beautiful old tree,
Sways in the wind,
Shedding tears of the time,
Season by season passes,
Unnoticed by mankind.

Young little trees,
Grow by her side,
And flowers with buzzing bees,
Popping in and out like the tide.

As she sheds her tears again,
She desperately hopes those little men,
Will remember her when,
They plant a new tree in her place,
As she leaves all her grace.

Sophie Clifford-Sanghad (11)
St John's RC Primary School

The Tiger

His stripes are as black as night,
And eyes green as grass.
And his smile is as pleasing as pretty girls.
But beware, beware his cunning smile.
Because all he wants is a light snack not
Friendship.

As he lowers you into his den
He smiles a sly smile.
And then you know, it's dinner time.

Niamh Egan (9)
St John's RC Primary School

OLD DOG

He stands slanted with an ache in his back
Alone on the lonely pavement.
There is a sad look in his brown old eyes
He staggers and then he falls.

The strangest moaning noise comes from him.
His coat is not fluffy but solid and bald -
You can feel his spine.
With movement his shoulders creak.
He won't live much longer you can tell
I even know that.
I will always hear that creaking groaning noise
As he slips away along the lonely pavement
Gone.

Sarah Tukmachi (9)
St John's RC Primary School

UNITED VS PALACE

United score
Palace snore
Rubbish skill
Neville ill
Crowd cheer
Men have beer
Crowd on the pitch
Johnsen gets an itch
Palace for the ball
Pallister tall
Beckham shoots
Nasty boots.

Jonathan J Williams (10)
St John's RC Primary School

BADGER

Softly walking up the lawn
Black and white striped head,
A graceful stride,
A soft look.

Sniffing, snuffling,
Looking for food,
Nose digging in the ground.
He's found a worm.

Suddenly a noise is heard,
The badger is gone,
All you see is a small
Tail and he carries on,
And disappears into the darkness.

Harriette Perkins (10)
St John's RC Primary School

TIGER

The tiger's feet beating
the ground
as it smashes the trees
its beautiful
eyes like a
fire
its claws shine
in the sun as it hunts
for its prey
it runs like the wind blows
and pounds on its one
victim.

Matthew Demichele (11)
St John's RC Primary School

AEROPLANE

I am the aeroplane
I go up high
I see the clouds
In the sky
But when I go
Down I see the
People under me
But I am so high
People look up and up
As high as they can look
People go on me
Girls, boys
Ladies and gentlemen
I like seeing my friends
It's fun
They know my name
Jumbo's my name
They shout out
Jumbo, Jumbo
Come and play with me
I can't said I, I'm on
Patrol.

Bernadette Kelly (11)
St John's RC Primary School

THE RAT

Little yellow eyes
Creeping through the frosty night
Beware the black rat.

Peter Thompson (8)
St John's RC Primary School

Eight Lives To Go

It happened in Reading Way,
To Kitty 'Pooh' one fateful day.
Knocked down by some passing lorry,
Left our 'Pooh' both sad and sorry.

To help poor Kitty in distress,
Appeared our Jane - air hostess.
A kindly and friendly maid,
Giving bandages and first-aid.

Words of sympathy were spoken,
Happily no bones were broken.
This story has a happy ending,
At hospital Kitty's mending.

Lucy Penfold (10)
St John's RC Primary School

Dresses

Dresses are everywhere.
Black is a nice colour for one,
So is red, green or blue or even some
Purple here or there.
People like dresses, I know I do.
Dresses - posh ones, thin ones,
Long ones, fat ones, nice ones,
But they're all dresses that's
What matters.
When I go shopping I wish
I could buy one but they
Just cost too much.

Samantha Peart (11)
St John's RC Primary School

School

School is good
School is bad
School has rules that make you go mad
Teachers teach
Children play
Teachers' nightmares are out in the yard
While children punch each other very hard.
The teachers yell
While the children shout
But who said the teachers
Have to take them out.
The bell goes for play
And there's a big shout
While the stampede of children
Comes roaring out.
The teachers go
And drink mouldy tea
We children mess about
But we still like
The teachers taking
Us out.

Rhys Corkhill (10)
St John's RC Primary School

Cat

Crawling through the night
Mice and birds he will frighten
It's a crawling cat.

Adam Kingston (8)
St John's RC Primary School

WHALE

When the water's calm,
and the dawn is young, and the fish swim
in the sea,
a song singer slowly slides and skims
the slippery waves like a seagull swimming
in a cloud.
He sways in the wind of the
salty air, and smoothes his
silky skin.
As he waves his tail to greet the sun,
the drops fall off the end
like a cool waterfall on a summer's day.
And when the water's calm,
and the dawn is young, and the fish swim
in the sea,
Silence . . .

Fionnuala Durrant (10)
St John's RC Primary School

CROCODILES

As the thirsty animals risk life and death,
To get water from the Nile,
As the animals did not know,
There are a group of crocodiles in the dangerous
Nile.
These crocodiles come to shore,
And they see a small little boar,
As the crocodiles reach and kill the boar,
The heard of buffalo run through,
There goes their lunch!

Samuel Cranmer (10)
St John's RC Primary School

The Giant Giant Millipede

The giant giant millipede, came crashing through the town,
Sheds and hedges, walls and trees all came tumbling down.
The baby woke and began to yell, the dog began to bark.
The millipede ran on and on until it reached the park.

It ate the kiddies' see-saw, threw the sand round like confetti,
And after polishing off the slide, slurped the swings up
like spaghetti!

The giant giant millipede, came crashing through the town,
Sheds and hedges, walls and trees all came tumbling down.
All the children dropped their sweets, the grocer dropped his goods.
The millipede ran on and on till it reached little woods.

It ate a three course breakfast (and a few waitresses too)
Soon after it felt rather sick and made his way to the loo!

It emptied all the rubbish bins and tore up every tree,
Then he tip-toed home for lunch . . . at least that's what my
friend told me!

Catherine Clark (9)
St John's RC Primary School

Rain

Rain is pouring down
We jumped in puddles and laughed
The rain didn't stop.

Liam Hopkinson (9)
St John's RC Primary School

VICTORIAN TIMES

Little children,
Your life may be horrid
But don't give up.
Tomorrow will be much different.
Look up, forget your smog-filled lungs
Up there is your very own star.
When you look up, you smile;
When you look down the hole of the coal mine
That rats come up and graze your scarred skinny legs.
Soon you will be in a much happier place.
Forget the clasping, squeezing and crunching machines
All they can do is make things.
But you have feelings, use them to make
A better life.

Rachel Hawkins (10)
St John's RC Primary School

THE MAGIC BOX

I will put in the box,
A glow of a firefly,
A buzz of a bee,
The noise of the sea.
I will put in the box,
One of the lightest snowflakes,
A white horse.
I will put in the box,
A forest of rainbows
Stars twinkling,
A hiss of a snake,
A noise of music.

Daniel Holmes (10)
St John's RC Primary School

The Magic Box

I will put in the box,

The purr of a new-born kitten,
The splash of a new-born wave,
The chirp of a new-born chick.

I will put in the box,

A gallop of a white horse,
A taste of a chocolate nut,
A twirl of a Spanish dancer.

I will put in the box,

The sight of a white mountain,
The smell of a salty sea,
The smile of a little girl.

I will put in the box,

The sight of a bright red rose,
The curious stare of a serious tiger,
In the magic box my secrets sleep.

Katharine Tudor (10)
St John's RC Primary School

Sun

Big round yellow sun.
The heat and warmth you give us
It shines bright and strong.

Charlotte Perry (9)
St John's RC Primary School

The Magic Box

I will put in my box,
A roar of a dragon,
Four pussy cat paws,
A tail of a mouse,
And a dinosaur's jaw.

I will put in my box,
A voice of a bird,
A parrot's beak,
A frog's toe,
And a bat's wing.

I will put in my box,
A snake's head,
A rat's nail,
A witch's nose,
And a rabbit's fluffy tail.

Amy Dyte (9)
St John's RC Primary School

The Beach

Gentle breeze blowing through the clouds.
All the gentle waves splashing around.
The golden sand blowing round and round.
The sun rises through that golden beach.
And then that gentle sea becomes heat.
Then sadness comes around.
The clouds become dark and rain drips become in different parts.
Then the country morn comes to that golden beach.
And then those gentle waves come to reach.

Graziella Di G'ati (10)
St John's RC Primary School

A Certain Little Victorian

Keep praying, keep hoping,
Don't listen to the voices of the rich
Try hard, dear child.
Believe in the power of God
He might, some day, help your fraying
little life.
I know that you envy the lives of the rich.
But just ignore them, dear child.
It could help you. Help you forget your fraying
little life.
Never let your smog filled lungs die out,
Let you down, give you away.
It just might help you. Help you ignore your
fraying little life.
I'll help you, if you want me to. Look into the future,
but, not into the past.
Just let your mind relax and things might just
get better. Just try. Please try.
I know your life is poverty-stricken. It's dead
and limp. But I can help you. Help you to say
goodbye to your fraying little life.

Sarah Heatley (10)
St John's RC Primary School

Alligator

Watch out here he comes
Crawling through the everglades
Menacing reptile!

Lucia Magee (9)
St John's RC Primary School

WINTER

One night it started snowing
The water was turning to ice
Like an ice-skating rink.
Snow covered the trees and grass.
It looked like the North Pole
with dogs covered in snow
like a polar bear.
Children were playing the next
morning on Christmas Eve,
having snow fights and snowballs
flying through the air.
As the three kids were walking
across the snow just like the
Three Kings did long ago.

Adrain Dennett (10)
St John's RC Primary School

THE SNAKE AND THE COUNTER

I'm pink and blue and your colour's blue too
I'm the longest of the snakes, 99 to 21
Come over here
I have Ritz hotel meals for two
We will waltz all night
We will waltz to the Blue Danube
We will drink red wine
We will watch the sun go down
We will have every little luxury
We will ride away on the white horses.
And then,

I will eat you.

Rachael Morton (10)
St John's RC Primary School

The Magic Box

I will put in the box,
The sound of country life,
A sunny, sandy beach,
The taste of chocolate ice-cream.

I will put in the box,
Chocolate that will last forever,
A rainbow that will never end,
The first ripple of life.

I will put in the box,
A picture of heaven,
A never-ending story,
A sunset like magic moonbeams.

I will put in the box,
A laugh that will never end,
A touch of a baby's face,
A touch of a smooth hedgehog.

I will put in the box,
A feel of a baby's hand or feet,
The first joy in the world,
The last sigh of a human.

Elizabeth Creevy (10)
St John's RC Primary School

Spiders

Long legged spider
Spinning pretty silky webs
On a nice long branch.

Charlotte Moon (8)
St John's RC Primary School

The 12 Days Of Christmas

On the 12th day of Christmas Marks & Spencer's
gave to me:

12 ripped jeans,
11 white shirts,
10 Easter eggs,
9 discount vouchers,
8 dirty vests,
7 gift vouchers,
6 boring books,
5 stuffed turkeys,
4 chocolate bars,
3 escalators,
2 hundred pounds
and
a sample of deodorant from them all!

Daniel Scullane (9)
St John's RC Primary School

My Life As A Donkey

I stagger along a twisting dry sandy path -
My eyes glint in the silver-lit moonlight.
Everything is silent, as silent as an eagle catching its prey.
The smell of rich water surrounds me,
A fiery golden circle rises from the golden sparkling sea
As a dove swoops from above me,
Spreading peace everywhere.
Then I enter a sandy desert.
My legs collapse onto the sandy desert,
And then everything comes to an end and I die.

Susan Westaway (10)
St John's RC Primary School

SPRING IS HERE!

Spring is here!
The ponds are clear.
Tortoises come out from their long winter sleep.
April showers give them a bath,
Squirrels are out and nibbling nuts.

Spring is here!
Flowers are here!
New life has come
Woolly lambs gallop alongside their mum
The world is full of germination.

Spring is here!
The sky is clear
The air is full of pollen
People get hay fever
Cricket has started
Tennis will start soon
Animals and life are everywhere!
Spring is here!

Julia Summerfield (10)
St John's RC Primary School

SNAKES

Snakes are slithering
Animals are shivering
Snakes' fangs are biting.

Matilda Judd (9)
St John's RC Primary School

PEACE

I can hear laughter, happiness
Then 11.00 strikes,
Two minutes' silence.
A little girl laughs, hasn't a care!
A little boy thinks, tries to remember
He pictures a time of war,
Unkindness, upsets,
Then two minutes is over,
He still pictures this time people arguing:
'It's unkind'
'It's our land'
'It's unkind'
'It's our land'
It repeats over and over,
He can't stand it anymore
That night he dreams,
He's evacuated away
A nightmare, could it be?
The next day he's up at Belgium.
Beautifully mown grass
Bright red poppies
He stays and thinks . . .

Joanne Benjamin (10)
St John's RC Primary School

THE SQUIRREL

It scampered past me
Then it disappeared from sight
It took my peanuts.

Charles Perry (9)
St John's RC Primary School

Black Cat

Black cat,
Glaring green eyes,
Staring up,
At a black night.
His only light is the moon,
Not a star, not a sun.
12 strikes,
Far far away
Midnight!
A leaf falls to the ground,
But does not dare to hurt silence.
Black cat,
Creeps on,
To attend his nightly business.

Charlotte Harrison (10)
St John's RC Primary School

Black Cat

When I see my friend's
black cat I wonder what
it's thinking.
Creeping around bushes,
its eyes glowing in the dark,
it moves mysteriously
under the full moon.
I see it clearly under the
dark sky.

Adam Hendry (9)
St John's RC Primary School

BLACK CAT

A black cat is fearless it isn't noisy
Its eyes are green and its paws are brown,
It's mostly sleeping.
It doesn't snore.
It's very clever too.
It does what you want it to do,
And it will help you
It can turn the TV on and off
It can change the channel.
And it will jump on you when you
Sleep.

George Youel (10)
St John's RC Primary School

POPPY BRIGHT

Poppy bright
Poppies breathe at night.
Played football
And shared a meal.
Poppy red shining,
And a blazing strength
And armour golden spirit and
Soul
Crying graves
Widow lady,
And haunted
hearts and lives.

Jeremy Todd (10)
St John's RC Primary School

THE MAGIC BOX

I will put in the box
Winnie the Pooh, honey
and friends.
I will put in the box
the noise of the sea
and a scare of a lion
a swirl of milkshake.
I will put in the box
a luxury of food
and a box of sweets
a roll of magazines
and diamonds too.
I will put in the box
the best make of
trainers in the world.

George West (10)
St John's RC Primary School

BLACK CAT

Black cat of the night
You strike me with your blackness.
You stare at me with your beady eyes.
You look up at me with them.
Your movement is as graceful as ever,
Your claws as big as needles,
Tell me why you strike me with your claws?
You lick me with your gripping tongue.
Your look is as lovely as night,
Your eyes as big as marbles,
Your eyes glow in the dark.

Amie Cooper (10)
St John's RC Primary School

Moses

On the Nile
In a basket
Made of weed,
There was a child
That child, with no name
Alone in that basket,
He flowed down the river
To the palace garden.
The princess heard him crying
She called her maid
So that she could have a son,
A son from that Nile.
She named him Moses
That meant one who came from water
He went and lived in the palace.

Michelle Holmes (9)
St John's RC Primary School

Myself

I am fiery like the sunset in the early morning
I am not at all shy like the white moon that
only appears in the night.
I think that I shall go on forever
like an everlasting stream.
I like to be wild like the wind on a cliff-top
in the early morning.
I am always there like an everlasting
piece of scenery.

Alexandra Chorley (11)
St John's RC Primary School

Comet

Icy, fast, hot dust
With its long, yellow, red tail
Into the night sky.

Nathan Collins (9)
St John's RC Primary School

The Mole

Mole snuffle and scratch
Digging your way in the dark
Mole with soft grey fur.

Antonia Schwartz (9)
St John's RC Primary School

Gold

Its shining hard coat
Found in its mine in moist soil
And dug up by us.

Richard Jones (8)
St John's RC Primary School

Colours Of Day

Flowers are happy,
They cover the fields with joy,
They are colourful.

Talitha Alexander (8)
St John's RC Primary School

Light

Bright moon give us light,
Sun shine on through the daytime,
Hale Bopp soars through stars.

Emma Proctor (9)
St John's RC Primary School

The Night Sky

The night sky is dark,
The moon is shining brightly,
Shadows are creepy.

Henrietta Forsyth (9)
St John's RC Primary School

The Rain

We need some more rain
Everything is drying up
The flowers are dead.

Edmund Mills (9)
St John's RC Primary School

Shining Flowers

Shining sunflowers
Dandelions and bluebells
Shining daffodils.

Sudevi Geary (8)
St John's RC Primary School

Earth

Thirsty the earth's ground
Dying for a drop of rain
Plants drying, earth cracked.

Victoria Clifford-Sanghad (9)
St John's RC Primary School

Spring

A horse just been born.
A brand new start for nature.
Spring is here again.

Hannah Piekarski (8)
St John's RC Primary School

Night

The moonlight shivers,
The sunlight has said goodbye,
And now it is night.

Hayley Morton (9)
St John's RC Primary School

A Rainbow

A rainbow in flight
Touches an open flower
To find gold nectar.

Thomas Wells (9)
St John's RC Primary School

Sun

The sunset at night
It's yellow and orange.
It shines everywhere.

Jamie Pethick (8)
St John's RC Primary School

The Titanic

In the cold of the North Atlantic,
A great ship passes by.
The huge iron bow cuts through the deep blue waters,
A gigantic island of ice cuts the waters too.
The ship and the ice move closer together,
Suddenly *bang!* The ship vibrates with the shriek of
Twisting metal.
A massive hole has been ripped open in the hull,
The screams of the passengers is deafening,
The ice-cold water is gushing into the first and
second flotation holds.
For eleven hours, the distressed ship lies slowly settling
into the water,
The lifeboats are launched.
Men and women struggling to escape from the iron
death trap,
Families separated and crying.
The rescued passengers look back, their luggage
and their future down the plug hole.

Sam Tree (11)
St John The Evangelist CEVA Primary School

The Man

There's a man down our road
he's very, very quiet
When you talk to him he grunts.
There's a man down our road
I'm scared of him
I wish he would go away
There's a man down our road
he smokes and drinks
and smells real bad
I wish he would go away
That man down our road
died today
I wish he'd come back
So I could say sorry.

Daniel Davies (9)
St John The Evangelist CEVA Primary School

My Mum

Thank you mum
for things you say
thank you mum for being there
thank you for your love and care.

Thank you mum
for all your hugs
and thank you mum for
being a friend
Giving a smile
and helping to make my day worthwhile.

Jenny Somers (10)
St John The Evangelist CEVA Primary School

Sound Of The Sea

The waves crashing,
The sea smashing,
These are the sounds of the sea.

Horses galloping,
Their tails wrapping,
Over the waves,
These are the sounds of the sea.

In the distance I hear them sing,
Mermaids sitting on the rocks,
These are the sounds of the sea.

Splashing of tails,
In the sea,
These are the dolphins I can see,

I laugh and giggle with glee,
As I hear the sounds of the wonderful
Sea, sea, sea.

Karen Waterson (10)
St John The Evangelist CEVA Primary School

Crocodile

Crocodiles, gliding, swiftly, curling, swirling, getting
closer and closer opening his jaws then suddenly *snap*
tails swishing tongues licking it's all over
Just a carcass is left the victim is dead.

Matthew Rawlinson (10)
St John The Evangelist CEVA Primary School

Remembrance Day

The fear, the death, the gloom,
The desolate feeling of doom,
Relatives gone off to fight,
No comfort in the candlelight,
The War,
Churned up earth and billowing smoke,
Hiding the enemy like a cloak,
No way to go home,
Chilled to the bone,
The War,
So remember today what happened back then,
The frightened child, the soldier, the wren,
They lost their lives, so now we have ours,
We think of them on . . .
Remembrance Day.

Jeremy Brice (10)
St John The Evangelist CEVA Primary School

Remember

Remember today those who gave
their lives
Remember the thousands who
tried to survive
Children playing in the road until they hear
the sirens go
Down in the shelter cold and dark
then they see a little spark.
Fighters going out to sea I wish they didn't
have to leave me.

Matthew Mortimore (11)
St John The Evangelist CEVA Primary School

SAVE THE WHALE

Splash!
Diving down to its deep, dark, world,
Where everything's silent except for the waves,
crashing on the sandy shore above.
The whale glides deeper to where the murky water turns into a tranquil paradise of rainbow colours.
Swiftly, the whale swims slowly through a multi-coloured path of peaceful fish.
Clearing a path through the magical deep of the ocean bed.
A dark shadow passes, sending fish disappearing in every direction into tiny crevices of the coral wall.
The whale approaches, unaware of the danger.
With every graceful stroke the whale gets nearer,
But escapes as the glinting harpoon breaks through the shimmering surface.
Save the whale!

Megan Pope & Nicola Adams (10)
St John The Evangelist CEVA Primary School

THE WHALE POEM

Whale, whale gliding through the sea
Whale, whale swimming free
Happy as can be
When suddenly the net drops
Making the whale stop
Whale, whale caught and slain
Was this really meant to be
Surely whales should be free.

Sarah Hotchkiss (10)
St John The Evangelist CEVA Primary School

MONSTER

There is a monster under the bed
It's big and hairy
There's a monster under the bed
it has three eyes and a slimy nose
There's a monster under the bed
It's green and orange and blue and red
There's a monster under the bed
My sister thinks I'm mad when I try to tell her that
there's a monster under the bed
When I told my mother she looked then she looked again she screamed and said
'There's a monster under the bed.'
It's a pity I didn't see it.

Rebbecca Davenport (10)
St John The Evangelist CEVA Primary School

MY PARENTS

Do your chores
Wash the dishes
Clean the windows
Feed the fishes
don't keep bugging me for a frog
I'm sure you would rather have a dog.
Before you go out brush
your hair and put away all the clothes
on your chair.
My parents are okay
Or are they?

Alice Moore (11)
St John The Evangelist CEVA Primary School

Remembrance Poem

Playing in the street,
throwing a ball.
Shuffling of feet,
Parents call.
Sirens go.
run inside,
Brother Joe,
don't go.
Lying on the floor,
screaming and dying,
closing that door,
seeing him crying.
That was so long ago,
but how it would be,
to see him again,
and live happily.

Holly Megilley (11)
St John The Evangelist CEVA Primary School

Splash

Splash, splash down goes his tail,
Look over there it's a whale.
As he goes over the crashing waves
in the water so blue.
Calling to his mum the sound sticks in my head
like glue.
He's coming over to me as I laugh and giggle with glee.
Its rubbery wet skin shining in the sunlight
Down beneath the sea it's a wonderful place to be
His sparkly blue eyes twinkling back at me.

Rebecca Locke (10)
St John The Evangelist CEVA Primary School

There Once Was A Chimpanzee

There once was a chimpanzee
Who swung from tree to tree.
But on the way home to have his tea.
A man shot the poor chimpanzee.

Adam Chetland (10)
St John The Evangelist CEVA Primary School

The Robin

Damp, dark, dingy day
I, the robin, came to play.
I flew across the misty moor
To find my breakfast,
Grubs galore.

My red breast glowed
To make me proud.
My song trilled loudly
In the boughs.
I played amongst the leaves all day,
When night time came, I flew away.

Elizabeth Thatcher (11)
The Royal School

I Wish

I wish I was a bird then I could sing
and I could fly and I could build my
home up high.

I wish I was an elephant
and carry passengers on my trunk.

I wish I was a little mouse
to scurry round the holes in the house.

I wish I was a beautiful butterfly
and then I could fly in the sky.

Sarah Case (10)
Walton Primary School

Animals And Pets

Lions roar
Tigers pound
Hyenas laugh
But I make no sound
(Sometimes)

Snakes hiss
Dogs bark
Hamster alone in the dark
Bears growl
Wolfves howl
But I make no sound.

Mark Hooper (10)
Walton Primary School

Rugby

Lineout
Scrums
That's the rugby
I know

Try
Conversion
That's the rugby
I know

Tall
Short
These are rugby players
I see

Stadiums
Big or small
These are stadiums
I see.

Daniel Sharp (10)
Walton Primary School

Man From Bulgaria

There was a young man from Bulgaria
who was suffering badly from malaria.
So he went to the doctor
and had a great shock there
because he'd never met anyone hairier anywhere.

Martin Critchlow (10)
Walton Primary School

My Dream World

Clear blue waters
Lots of trees
Clear blue skies
With fluffy little
Clouds
My dream world

Long green grass
Clear blue waves
And the hot, yellow
Sun shining on us
My dream world

Roaring lions
Scuttering ants
No creatures
Extinct
My dream world

No parents working
No children
At school
And best of all no
Homework
My dream world.

Sharon Evans (9)
Walton Primary School

Fish Freedom

In the sea
Creatures are great and small.
From whales to tiny fish.
It's time they moved on because
of the fisherman.
As they use their
Song to move from
left to right.
Being strong on their way.
They reach a bay
Scrounge around at
the shallow end of
the water for little bugs.
Making sure they get
every scrap before
moving on again.

Ryan John Heal (10)
Walton Primary School

Night Fright

Swirling flames of
Red and orange
Billowing smoke
Into the sky,
The smell of ash
Is all around
You, as the fright,
Of the night,
Goes by.

Sally Kemp (10)
Walton Primary School

MY WORLD

In my world it would be like a dream
A lovely, lovely running stream
Animals wandering all about
No mums or dads around to shout.
No forests cut down they're there to stay.
Creatures safe
Just there to play.
No school
No work
No ghoul
No smirks
Always peace and quiet.

Wouldn't it be wonderful
If I had a world of my own.
No grans or grandads around to moan
Don't need to buy
Don't need to sell
Everyone's safe everyone's well.

Charlotte Tracey (10)
Walton Primary School

SPANISH LIMERICK

There was an old lady from Spain.
Who suffered from varicose veins.
So she got in her car.
Unfortunately didn't get far.
Because she had terrible pains.

Rebecca Kibblewhite (10)
Walton Primary School

I Want A Dog

What animal do you think
would make a brilliant pet?
Susie said a rat
Mark said ask a vet
Jamie said a fluffy playful cat
Gran said it would get fat
Dad said he won't have it
Mum said just be content with a rabbit
Grampa said go get a goldfish
Nan said but then you'll have to buy a dish
But I just want a
Dog

Stacey Davies (10)
Walton Primary School

Somerset

S ometimes it is so quiet.
O nly the sound of silence.
M um said, 'It is great here.'
E veryone else says that too.
R abbits run in the wind.
S heep graze peacefully.
E veryone's special dream.
T his place is paradise.

Simon Hasnip (11)
Walton Primary School

Another Bird Is Homeless

One night a terrible storm
Blew over some trees
Bash! Crash! Smash!
Another bird is homeless

Man with a saw
Chops down some trees
Bash! Crash! Smash!
Another bird is homeless

A digger trundled along
Dug up some trees
Bash! Crash! Smash!
Another bird is homeless

Water gushes along
Sinks some trees
Bash! Crash! Smash!
Another bird is homeless.

Owen Eades (10)
Walton Primary School

Homeless

High in the treetops
Way up there
A monkey sits
Unaware
A man with a saw
Comes along
Another monkey loses his home.

Jessica Barnicoat (10)
Walton Primary School

INFORMATION

We hope you have enjoyed reading this book - and that you will continue to enjoy it in the coming years.

If you like reading and writing poetry drop us a line, or give us a call, and we'll send you a free information pack.

Write to :-

Young Writers Information
1-2 Wainman Road
Woodston
Peterborough
PE2 7BU
(01733) 230748